r w nales

Kate Riggs

CREATIVE EDUCATION
CREATIVE PAPERBACKS

seedlings

Published by Creative Education and Creative Paperbacks
P.O. Box 227, Mankato, Minnesota 56002
Creative Education and Creative Paperbacks
are imprints of The Creative Company
www.thecreativecompany.us

Design by Ellen Huber; production by Joe Kahnke
Art direction by Rita Marshall
Printed in China

Photographs by Alamy (Arco Images GmbH, phil gould, Karina
Walton), Getty Images (Design Pics Inc.), iStockphoto (pilipenkoD),
Minden Pictures (Hiroya Minakuchi), National Geographic Creative
(HIROYA MINAKUCHI/MINDEN PICTURES, PAUL NICKLEN,
RICH REID), Shutterstock (Chris Curtis, Tatiana Ivkovich, Mike
Liu, Benny Marty, Christopher Meder, Christian Musat, Mike
Price), SuperStock (John Hyde/Alaska Stock - Design Pics)

Library of Congress Cataloging-in-Publication Data
Names: Riggs, Kate, author.
Title: Killer Whales / Kate Riggs.
Series: Seedlings.
Includes index.
Summary: A kindergarten-level introduction to killer whales,
covering their growth process, behaviors, the oceans they call
home, and such defining features as their black-and-white
coloration.
Identifiers: LCCN 2016054476 / ISBN 978-1-60818-869-7
(hardcover) / ISBN 978-1-62832-484-6 (pbk) / ISBN 978-1-
56660-917-3 (eBook)

Subjects: LCSH: Killer whale—Juvenile literature.
Classification: LCC QL737.C432 R555 2017 / DDC 599.53—dc23

CCSS: RI.K.1, 2, 3, 4, 5, 6, 7;
RI.1.1, 2, 3, 4, 5, 6, 7; RF.K.1, 3; RF.1.1

First Edition HC 9 8 7 6 5 4 3 2 1
First Edition PBK 9 8 7 6 5 4 3 2 1

TABLE OF CONTENTS

Hello, killer whales!

The killer whale lives in cold oceans. A layer of fat called blubber keeps it warm.

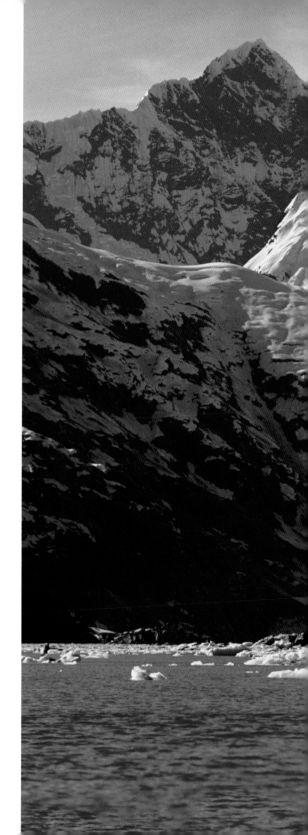

Black-and-white killer whales have two flippers. A fin is on the back.

Killer whales breathe air. They use a blowhole to breathe.

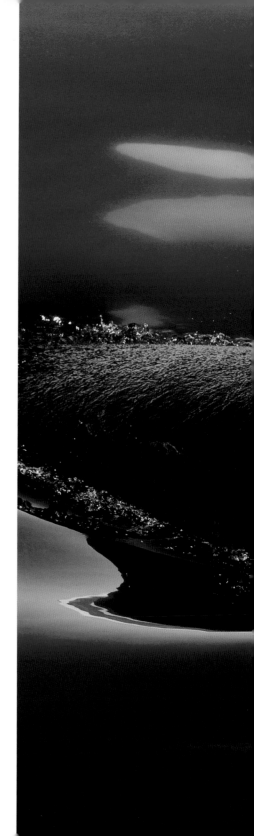

This is on top of the head.

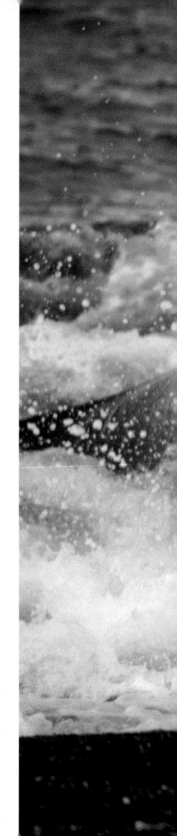

Killer whales are hunters. They hunt in groups. Killer whales eat fish and other sea animals.

A calf is a baby killer whale.

It grows and grows.

Calves live with their families.

Pods of killer whales stay together. They swim from place to place. They click and whistle to each other.

Goodbye, killer whales!

Picture a Killer Whale

saddle patch

tail

tail flukes

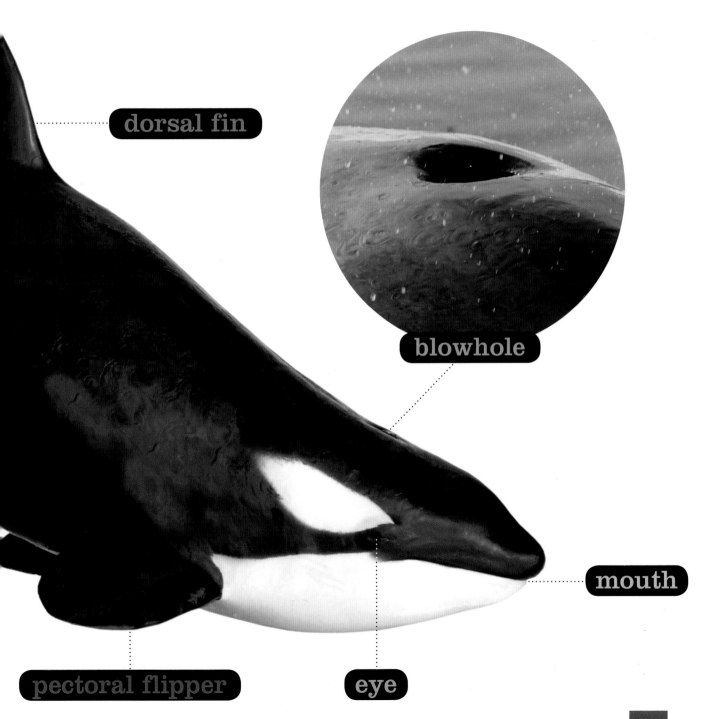

dorsal fin

blowhole

mouth

pectoral flipper

eye

Words to Know

flippers: flat limbs (like arms) that help killer whales swim

oceans: big areas of deep, salty water

pods: family groups of killer whales

Read More

Heos, Bridget. *Do You Really Want to Meet an Orca?*
Mankato, Minn.: Amicus, 2016.

Riggs, Kate. *Killer Whales.*
Mankato, Minn.: Creative Education, 2012.

Websites

Enchanted Learning: Orca or Killer Whale
http://www.enchantedlearning.com/subjects/whales/activities/whaletemplates/Orcatemp.shtml
Find out more information, and print a picture to color.

National Geographic Kids: Orca
http://kids.nationalgeographic.com/animals/orca/#orca-jumping.jpg
Learn more about killer whales, or orcas.

Index